BLESSINGS

JEREMY P. TARCHER/PUTNAM

a member of Penguin Putnam Inc.

New York

BLESSINGS

Prayers and

Declarations for a

Heartful Life

JULIA
CAMERON

Most Tarcher/Putnam books are available at special quantity discounts for bulk
purchases for sales promotions, premiums, fund-raising, and educational needs.
Special books or book excerpts also can be created to fit specific needs.
For details, write or telephone Putnam Special Markets,
200 Madison Avenue, New York, NY 10016; (212) 951-8891.

Jeremy P. Tarcher/Putnam
a member of
Penguin Putnam Inc.
200 Madison Avenue
New York, NY 10016
www.penguinputnam.com

Library of Congress Cataloging-in-Publication Data

Cameron, Julia.
Blessings: prayers and declarations for a heartful life / by Julia Cameron.
p.   cm.
ISBN 0-87477-906-5 (alk. paper)
1. Meditations.   2. Devotional calendars.   I. Title.
BL624.2.C34   1998   97-36670 CIP
291.4'32—dc21

Printed in the United States of America
9   10

This book is printed on acid-free paper. ∞

Book design by Claire Naylon Vaccaro

For those

who are

our companions

INTRODUCTION

Life is a creative endeavor. It is active, not passive. We are the yeast that leavens our lives into rich, fully baked loaves. When we experience our lives as flat and lackluster, it is our consciousness that is at fault. We hold the inner key that turns our lives from thankless into fruitful. That key is "Blessing."

"My father's house has many mansions," we are told. By counting our blessings, we name ourselves accurately as children of the universe, the richly dowried children of God, or, if you prefer, of "good." Focused on our good, focused on our abundance, we naturally attract more of the same. This is spiritual law. Our consciousness is creative. What we focus on, we empower and enlarge. Good multiplies when focused upon. Negativity multiplies when focused upon. The choice is ours: Which do we want more of?

In every event, in every circumstance, we have a choice of perspective. Faced with difficulty, we can choose between disappointment and curiosity as our mind-set. The choice is ours. Will we focus on what we see as lacking or will we look for the new good that is emerging? In every moment, however perilous or sorrowful it may feel, there is the seed of our greater happiness, greater expansion, and greater abundance.

It is easy to bless events that coincide with our perceived good. When things are going "our way," it is easy to experience faith and gratitude. To bless what might be called "contrary" circumstances requires more faith. Things do not seem to be going our way. In fact, the flow of events may actually run counter to our desires. In all times of such apparent difficulty, it is crucial to bless the flow of events as right and appropriate despite our reservations. The delays, difficulties, and disruptions we experience can in this way enlarge and enrich us. In short, we bless not only the road but the bumps on the road. They are all part of the higher journey.

It is easy, too, to bless people who are sunny and harmonious. It is easy to perceive such personalities as blessings on our path. When people are stormy and temperamental, when people are withholding, mean-spirited, greedy, or judgmental, it is more difficult to bless them, more difficult to perceive their positive contribution to our path. Faced with such unhappy individuals, blessing allows us to lessen their negative impact, to remember that they hold no real power over us. Blessing reminds us that our dignity comes from a divine source. That source is the wellspring of our self-valuing.

The key to practicing blessings is the willingness to accept the full value of each moment. As we are willing to allow each difficult moment to soften and transform into its inner potential, our hearts become hopeful, clear, brave. As we extend the tendrils of our faith above and through the walls of our resistance, our lives become green, verdant, affirming. We are the wild rose basking in the sun. As we cling to our conscious optimism, finding footholds of faith despite opposition, our lives become rooted in the soil of grace. We are nurtured, prospered, and blessed.

The act of blessing is a step into faith. Rather than stand blocked or stymied by circumstances that appear adversarial, we step forward, claiming the safety of our path, the firmness of the soil of God. We affirm, "This is to my benefit. This circumstance blesses my life; I am grateful to this difficult situation for the many gifts it carries. I accept my blessings as they unfold within me."

Counting every blessing is a small step in the direction of our dreams. We gradually perceive our lives on a safe and protected path. Every time we recognize a blessing, it increases our capacity to receive a blessing.

As we expand our consciousness in gratitude, we become larger vessels for good. We can consciously and creatively choose to count and encounter our good. We can consciously and creatively choose to expand.

This is easier than it may sound—easier even in the face of very real and very human difficulties.

Blessing a difficulty is not simply accepting it. It is looking at it with new eyes, considering it from a higher, more open-minded perspective. To bless a situation is not to deny its sorrowful or challenging reality. To bless a situation is to claim its inner, hidden reality, a higher, finer working-out of good for all concerned.

To bless a difficult situation, we must soften our hearts to it. When we are in the pain of a difficult realization, we tend instead to wince and steel our hearts against acceptance. We feel the prodding of a pointed awareness and we recoil, fearing it is the point of a lance that will pierce us through.

Blessing is the scalpel of spiritual healing. It removes our poisoned attitudes of fear and constriction, causing the infection of self-importance to flow away, leaving us surrendered and open to the healing action of spirit, the cleansing power of grace. As we surrender resistance, we open our hearts. Freed to love again, they become full, expansive, and wise. We are no longer victimized by resentment and anger. A higher hand is at work.

I take a daily walk with my dogs through a mesa of sagebrush near my house. It was on one of those walks that the idea for this book came to me. It came in the form of what I call my "Marching Orders," what others might call "the still, small voice." One moment I was walking through the sage, breathing in its sweet, heavy scent and enjoying the still-snowcapped mountains that ring Taos valley. The next moment I was "listening" to a startling new direction for my work: I was to write a book of "lessons." Those lessons would concern an attitude of gratitude, of thankfulness for gifts received.

By now I am used to receiving such creative directives. My walks, in fact, are intended to invite them, but this one surprised me. I already had my writing plans for the next year. Just when did the Guidance think this book would get written and what made it think that I could write it? No sooner had these doubts surfaced than the firm inner voice persisted, "This is what you are to do *now*, next."

I went home and called my editor.

"I know we think we know what I am writing," I began. "But evidently there is something else that I am supposed to do first."

I told my editor the book that had been outlined on my walk.

"So we'll do it," he said.

The book you hold in your hands is that little book. My experience of writing it was one of near anonymity. The prayers and declarations came to me not as things to be written but as things to be written down. I did not so much write this book as transcribe it. I learned from it as I wrote. What I learned is the importance of a practice that Buddhists call "mindfulness," the cherishing of each moment. I prefer the term "heartfulness," as it more closely describes the direction of the lessons that I was given.

May this book yield you a more heartful life.

BLESSINGS

To bring forth the soul of our being, we must be in our
bodies, rooted to Earth, able to draw from the
universal source of energy.

DIANE MARIECHILD

THIS EARTH IS RADIANT
WITH GRACE

The world is abundant. It is filled with beauty. The world holds abundant beauty in people, things, and events. The world offers abundant supply for my every need in people, things, and events. In this generous world, my needs are met through many sources. My desires are fulfilled through many channels. This world is sacred, bountiful, and generous. I recognize and appreciate this abundance. I have the courage to desire my good and I have the expectations of my good being fulfilled. I am partnered and provided for by universal flow. I am enriched by universal supply. Carefully and consciously, I am cared for in earthly ways by divine sources. My good is assured. I prosper in this abundant world.

God, I can push the grass apart
And lay my finger on Thy heart.

EDNA ST. VINCENT MILLAY

A BROAD AND RADIANT RIVER OF GOODNESS FLOWS SURELY THROUGH MY LIFE

Divine flow prospers my endeavors. Divine supply funds my dreams. I open my heart to divine action in all my affairs. I am ready and able to act on divine guidance as it unfolds within me and outside of me in every circumstance. When I am lonely and overwhelmed, I remind myself I am partnered by a loving universe. I turn my attention inward, seeking a state of calm. I listen both within and without for promptings—signs, signals, and communications—that ease my soul and allow it to act wisely and decisively.

MY HEART IS A WISE
AND FAITHFUL GUIDE

I bless the wisdom of my loving heart. Love is a form of listening. I listen with a loving heart. I listen to the love within my heart and I hear the love in the hearts of others. My heart guides me tenderly and truly. I find ways through the wilderness. My heart finds paths through the desert. My heart is valiant and wise. My heart senses the truth and offers compassion in times of conflict. My heart has patience. My heart has humility. It is fully human and fully divine. As I listen to my heart, I am able to love humanly with divine wisdom. I am wiser than I know, kinder than I believe. I am loving and compassionate to others and myself. My heart holds the world in tender awe.

*All you need to do to receive guidance is
to ask for it and then listen.*

SANAYA ROMAN

I TRUST MY INNER WISDOM

I consciously validate my perceptions. I count myself as a valuable, insightful, and objective observer of life. Looking at my life and my situation, I applaud my capacity for wise choices, discerning actions. I am more clear-eyed and perceptive than I have often thought. At this time I consciously recall situations in which my own clarity and sense of the unfolding of events were borne out to be true and accurate. Rather than focus on the times when I have made mistakes or suffered errors of judgment, I focus instead on the many times when I have seen clearly, acted properly, and been rewarded for my wisdom by a happy unfolding of events. My acuity is a great blessing for me and others.

The light which shines in the eye is really the light of the heart. The light which fills the heart is the light of God.

RUMI

MY WORLD IS A WORLD OF LOVE AND MY LOVE IS A LOVING WORLD

My heart is a home for God. God is a home for my heart. I am large enough to hold God's entire world within me. I am small enough that God's entire world holds me also in its heart. There is no separation between hearts. There is no distance. Love is the substance of all life. Everything is connected in love, absolutely everything. When I focus my heart on the love of a person, I am connected to that person. As I open to compassion and freedom for others, I find compassion and freedom for myself. We are all loved. We are all loving. We are all love seeking to express itself in love and in so doing receive love in return. When I listen to love, I am listening to my true nature. When I express love, I am expressing my true nature. All of us love. All of us do it more and more perfectly. The past has brought us both ashes and diamonds. In the present we find the flowers of what we've been and the seeds of what we are becoming. I plant the seeds of love in my heart. I plant the seeds of love in the hearts of others. We are God's garden, as God is our own. Our garden grows more beautiful as we recognize and realize who we are. We are love becoming more loving, becoming more loved as we know who we are. I love the world and those I share it with. The world I share shares love.

You must remember that man is noble, man is sublime, man is divine, and can accomplish whatever he desires.

SWAMI MUKTANANDA

I OPEN MY HEART TO LOVE WITH AN OPEN HAND

My gift for unconditional love is a great blessing in my life. I am able to manifest an inner nobility in my relationships. I accept those who love me as they are. I allow them to love me at their speed and tempo as they are able. I do not dictate or control. Their love for me is a gift. I allow them the right to choose how and when they can give it. Those who love me are part of God's love for me. They are a part of the larger plan of my life. I allow God to remain the whole. I root myself in God, accepting the relationships which come to me as a part of something larger that holds all of us within its scope. I find the steadiness of divine companionship. I allow God to be my primary security, the deep soil of my heart's safety. Rooted in God, I allow human love to gift me and grace me but I do not demand a godlike security from human love. I find perfect love, perfect security, and perfect safety in God. I allow my human loves to be human and I love them in their humanity.

MY FRIENDSHIPS ARE GROUNDED IN GOD

My love is sourced by divine love, shaped by divine guidance, prospered by divine power. I cherish my friendships. Rooted in God, they are flexible and enduring. They are honest, heartfelt, and healthy. I maintain deep affections without fear of abandonment. Knowing all souls are part of God and God is part of all souls, I see my friends as divine in nature and origin while human in form. Recognizing our divine origins, I am serene and secure in the underlying communion of grace in which we dwell.

All life is vibration. You combine with what you notice, or
you combine with what you vibrate to. If you are vibrating
to injustice and resentment you will meet it on your
pathway, at every step.

FLORENCE SCOVEL SHINN

I AM OPENHEARTED
AND EXPANSIVE

I am blessed with a hospitable heart. I welcome new souls into my family of souls. I open my heart to new companions. I am a field warm with the sun. My grasses wave green and abundant. As I welcome new life, my heart blossoms with new flowering. New friendships, new experiences, new thoughts, ideals, and insights come to me as I practice openhearted acceptance of life's abundant gifts. As my life expands in volume and velocity, I remind myself that God is the ground of my being. All people and events are rooted in divine consciousness. All unfold together for my greater good. Even as I welcome the new, I salute and release the old. I allow people and events to pass from my sphere, wishing them well, wishing them love and fulfillment on their journey. All that I have loved, I do love. My heart expands to allow greater and greater freedom to those whom it loves. My heart blesses its beloveds with the double gift of freedom and connection.

The history of the world is none other than the progress
of the consciousness of freedom.

GEORG HEGEL

MY FREEDOM IS THE GATEWAY TO A LARGER LIFE

I cherish my freedom to act, think, feel, and choose as I wish. I celebrate the choice which lies for me in every moment. I accept the responsibility which comes with freedom. I embrace my liberty and use it to create an abundant and meaningful life. I gratefully acknowledge the expansive opportunities my freedom allows me. I recognize that the shape of my life can largely be of my own choosing. Knowing that I am free, accepting that I am free, relishing that freedom and using it to build a life built upon my true values, I am fortunate and know that that is so.

Today I do affirm that I am Divinely guided. . . . There is
That within which knows what to do and how to do it, and
It compels me to act on what It knows.

ERNEST HOLMES

I CO-CREATE MY LIFE
THROUGH CONSCIOUS
CHOICE

L ife is intentional, not accidental. I bless this central fact. Consciousness instigates shifts in outer reality. Recognizing that I have the power to change my world by changing my thinking, I set for myself a gentle vigilance toward negative thoughts. When I fear abandonment, I remind myself that the universe itself is my loving companion. When I fear stagnation, I surrender into the deeper flow of life rather than willfully forcing artificial solutions. Constantly partnered by an interactive universe, I do my part by reminding myself that I am part of a larger plan, partnered by an infinite intelligence. In its perfect pink blossoming, the bloom of the apple tree does not concern itself with whether a bee will appear. The blossom does its job just by blossoming. The bee is drawn to do the rest. Rather than imagine that my yearnings are self-centered or counter to the flow of life, I practice simply blossoming in the faith that I attract what I need simply by following and blessing my true nature.

*There is a vitality, a life force, an energy, a quickening, that
is translated through you into action, and because there is
only one of you in all time, this expression is unique.
And if you block it, it will never exist through any
other medium and will be lost.*

MARTHA GRAHAM

THE BREATH OF SPIRIT
BREATHES THROUGH ME

I am a unique conduit for the good of the universe
to flow into the world. As I listen and respond to
my inner guidance, I bring to the world originality
and opportunity. I have a unique healing presence
which blesses those who know me. As I open my heart
to being true to my own nature, I provide for others a
personal and providential medicine. We do not interact
by mistake. I am placed where I am and with whom I
am for many important reasons. As I become more

fully myself, my individual personality brings specific gifts to those who surround me. As I open myself to unfolding my own inner gifts, the gifts of my nature grace others in outward and material ways. My presence in this world is important. My attitudes and actions have importance. As I choose to be a healing and creative presence, I am a balm for a troubled world. The grace of Spirit touches me and through me touches all I encounter.

It is right and necessary that we should be individuals.
The Divine Spirit never made any two things alike—
no two rosebushes, two snowflakes, two grains
of sand, or two persons. We are all just a little unique
for each wears a different face; but behind each
is the One Presence—God.

ERNEST HOLMES

WE ARE PRECIOUS JEWELS
IN THE CROWN OF SPIRIT

Each of us is unique, valuable, worthy, and irre-placeable. Each of us is kind, wise, knowing, and gifted. Each of us is filled with dignity, gifted with humor, funded with strength. We are met as equals. We bear gifts for each other. Our hearts are true friends, true colleagues. We have a place with each other. We have a need for each other. All of us seek the same answers, although we find them by different routes. All of us hold the same questions although we express them in different ways. Our loving hearts hold the solutions all of us seek. This is a great blessing and indisputable fact. In loving each other, we love the world. In loving each other, we find the world. The world we find is healed by our loving hearts.

The world of reality has its limits;
the world of imagination is boundless.

JEAN-JACQUES ROUSSEAU

CQ

MY SOUL INHABITS MANY
WORLDS WITH COMFORT

D istance and diversity are part of me. I bless my width and depth. All that is foreign and unfamiliar is yet a part of who I am. Mine is the family of man. My tribe inhabits the earth, walking in different lands, speaking in different tongues but living one life as we go forward. Knowing that I am a part of all life, I cherish differences. I embrace diversity. Recognizing that all faces and forms are my own face and form, I treat myself and others with dignity. We are brothers. We are sisters. We are husband and wife, mother and father. We are a family of many colors and many cloaks. We are one life. The language of the heart speaks to us all. I cherish that which my brother cherishes. I walk in harmony, generosity, and abundance. I share my gifts from the gifts I share.

If you look deeply into the palm of your hand, you will see
your parents and all generations of your ancestors. All of
them are alive in this moment. Each is present in your body.
You are the continuation of each of these people.

THICH NHAT HANH

THE BLOOD OF LIFE
FLOWS THROUGH ME

We are not alone. We are privileged to carry in our blood and bone the wisdom of those who have gone before us. We carry their lives, even in the face of their deaths. In each of us there survive the lives of those who gave us life. In our children, and in our brainchildren, our own lives go forward. Faced with the loss of a human love, I turn to the divine love within me which can accept that loss, embrace that loss, and carry forward the beloved whom I feel to be beyond reach. God is in me and I am in God. All that ever was, still is. We are a divine energy, a divine life. In our dying, we live again. In our living, we die again. There is no loss which is not a gain carried forward. In my moments of greatest sorrow, I am touched by the joy of having loved. In my times of greatest loss, I am still loved. Love is not lost through loss. It is found more fully. I cherish the love my loss has helped me find.

People talk about nature. As the water moves, it makes its
own sound. As the wind blows, it makes its own sound.
When fire burns, it makes its own sound. In the same
way, all of us have that music going on.

SWAMI CHIDVILASANANDA

THE MELODY OF LIFE
FLOWS THROUGH ME

The song of life is infinite and variable. Its melodies and harmonies hold infinite possibilities. I am both the listener and the song. I am both the composer and the note. A creator myself, I am also the creation of a larger hand. In the great symphony of life, I am both large and small. I welcome this paradox. I allow myself to feel the protective guidance of a greater whole even as I allow myself to feel the power of my own largeness and strength. The balance is perfect, the design sublime. Recognizing that I am small enough to receive help and large enough to give it, I both receive energy and extend energy with a rhythm as melodic and as natural as breathing. Conscious of this process, I know that I can inhale greater support when that is my need, and exhale greater support when that is the need of others. My life is lived in harmony. I am a graceful note consciously and organically connected to the universal song. As I am true to myself, those who are in harmony with me resonate to my personality and come to my side. Knowing that, I count myself blessed. I find myself both powerful and protected.

We must be aware of the real problems of the world.
Then, with mindfulness, we will know
what to do and what not to do
to be of help.

THICH NHAT HANH

WE ARE TRUSTWORTHY STEWARDS OF OUR WORLD

The world is a work in progress. We are the architects of a better world. In our hearts, we hold compassion, invention, clarity, and hope. We know right action. We know wisdom. We know divine intent. The world is safe in our keeping. We are loving. We are wise. We are good. We can change our world for the better. We can bring our best to the world. The whole world lies within each of us. Our every thought and act touch all. I am powerful. We are powerful. As I make my inner world gentle, harmonious, and joyful, I bring those qualities to the world which all of us share. I cherish the world which we share. I bless the world and those I share it with.

I AM A VESSEL
FOR DIVINE ENERGY

y heart is a chalice for love. I am well loved. I open my heart to feel that I am loved. I allow myself to be saturated by love. I soften my heart and gently ask it to receive the love I encounter. I do not need to earn love. I do not need to work at love. I need only to allow myself to feel the love extended toward me. I need only to accept love to know that I am lovable. I choose to remember—and cherish—the ways in which I am loved.

For Mercy has a human heart,
Pity a human face,
And Love, the human form divine.

WILLIAM BLAKE

I LOVE OTHERS
FOR THEIR
TRUE SELVES

I bless and salute the divine goodness available for all human beings and in all human beings. I allow people to be uniquely themselves, bringing their true natures and true gifts to our relationships. I do not demand that those who love me change their essential nature for my comfort. I express to them my nature. I tell them my truth. I do not hide or pretend I am different from what I am. I trust that each of us is a perfect part of the divine whole. I trust that each of

us is as lovable as we are. I allow originality, inventive-
ness, and variability in my loving relationships. I invite
the unique souls in my life to love me as their true
selves allow.

Everyone has all things in himself and sees all things in another; so that all things are everywhere and all is all and each is all, and the glory is infinite.

PLOTINUS

⁂

I AM A FOUNTAIN
IN THE LIGHT

As I bless all I encounter, all I encounter blesses me. Joy and well-being pour forth from my contented heart. I am sourced by divine power. A divine force flows out from me into the world. All I encounter are touched by the divine spark within me. I am touched by the divine spark within all others. Meeting a stranger, I see the familiar face of God. Meeting adversity, I see the hidden face of God. There is no situation so foreign that I do not claim and recognize good working through it and in it.

When I encounter sorrow, I open my heart to contain and transform it. I allow the action of loving compassion to alchemize all difficulty into an opportunity to find the hidden face of God and cherish it.

At the height of laughter, the universe is flung into
a kaleidoscope of new possibilities.

JEAN HOUSTON

I ANTICIPATE GREAT GOOD
AND OPEN MY HEART TO IT

I am alert to new beginnings. I open my heart to bless the "hello" that comes to me uninvited and unexpected. I bring to my world a child's openness to new companions. I allow myself to be met. In the face of new beginnings, I practice curiosity and expansion. I embrace risk and I open to play. Mine is a festive heart. I do not allow old songs and old ideas to become the only melodies I will listen to. I practice a listening heart. I am attentive to the pipings of small adventures. Even in the face of haste, even in the light of past experience, I entertain optimism, allow enthusiasm, encourage care. My heart is resilient and expansive. I cherish all that I have and welcome my ability to care still further for all that yet is offered me.

Humor is not a mood but a way of looking at the world.

LUDWIG WITTGENSTEIN

The situation is critical . . . but not serious.

SONIA CHOQUETTE

MY HUMOR LIGHTS THE WORLD

I am blessed by wit and humor. I see the light side of dark times. I see the antic grace in awkwardness, the comic foibles in human nature. I am serious in my commitments but I am lighthearted in my fulfillment of them. I allow myself to feel the support of universal forces. This connection to spiritual reality allows me to move more lightly through the world. My laughter is a great bell blessing my life. My friendships are graced by humor and shared laughter. My spirituality is grounded in joy. Humor blesses my world.

Enthusiasm means "of the gods." When you have an enthusiastic heart, all the heavens can flow through it.

SONIA CHOQUETTE

MY ENTHUSIASM FUNDS ME WITH POWER

I am blessed by the gift of an enthusiastic heart. I respond to life with lively interest, with contagious joy, with ardor and delight. My enthusiasm is a spiritual wellspring. It graces me with energy. It fills me with passion and with the perseverance to see that passion out. My enthusiasm is a fuel for my endeavors. It is a fire which warms me and my friends. I greet the world with a lover's open heart. I do not allow cynicism or skepticism to sour my attitudes.

Why do you walk through the fields in gloves
When the grass is soft as the breasts of doves
And shivering sweet to the touch?

FRANCES CORNFORD

MY SENSE OF TOUCH GIFTS
ME WITH PLEASURE

I take pleasure in my sense of touch. It grounds me in the physical world. It connects me to my surroundings. The silken feel of a baby's hair, the sleek coat of a dog, the satiny feel of my lover's skin, the sleek hide of a horse—all these bring me pleasure. The cool blessing of water, the hot gift of soup, the warmth of the sun, the gentle touch of wind—all these grace me with their feel.

My sense of touch receives love and expresses it. My sense of love receives care and expresses it. My sense of touch allows my soul to meet the world intimately, sweetly, and with ardor. I bless my sense of touch and savor all that it brings to me.

The sky is the daily bread of the eyes.

RALPH WALDO EMERSON

MY SENSE OF SIGHT
CONNECTS ME TO MY WORLD

The exquisite line of a lover's hand, the graceful shape of an apple-laden bough dipping in the wind, the contour of a mountain's flank, the cottony fluff of a dandelion gone to seed—my eyes cherish these sights and many more. My child's first steps, my father's ailing walk, the dance of flowers windblown in a meadow—my eyes witness all of these.

I cherish the sights I behold. I savor the sights I see. My gift of sight brings me the gift of insight. I bless the vision brought to me by vision.

We are all, in a sense, music.

DON CAMPBELL

I AM A FLUTE FOR THE MUSIC OF GOD'S LOVE

I am a conduit for divine kindness to pour forth into the world. As I make of my heart a loving balm for those in difficulty, I find I, too, am soothed, for compassion pours out from me as a grace which heals me and heals others. There is no wound which does not benefit from human kindness. Compassion is divine in nature but human in expression. As I resolve to be a gateway for kindness to enter the world, I am led myself into a kinder world. As I extend myself in generosity and warmth, my world becomes warmer and more generous. The vessel of my heart is sourced in God. Drawing on this divine source, my supplies of love are boundless. Remembering that divine love loves through me, I am able to love freely and without exhaustion. Drawing on universal love, I am able to cherish others and myself.

*We are part of the vast continuum of existence that
includes all things conscious, unconscious, inert, physical,
mental, emotional, known and unknown, imaginable
and unimaginable.*

SUSAN BAKER

THE SEASONS OF MY HEART
HAVE PURPOSE AND
MEANING

I bless my connection to all that is. In times of
doubt and despair, I turn my attention to the natural world. Recognizing that all things have seasons of growth and birth, seasons of decay and
gestation, I allow myself to experience the cyclicality in
my own life. Where I experience loss, I anticipate future growth. Where I experience emptiness, I anticipate an inflow of the new. Where I experience doubt

and dismay, I welcome a resurgence of faith and conviction. I allow my life to be tidal. I allow my life to fill and empty according to a plan higher than I might naturally perceive. Out of my periods of drought and desolation, I affirm that new growth occurs, funded in deeper strength due to my times of testing and difficulty. It is all for the good, I remind myself. There is a purpose and a point to all I undergo. My pain engenders in me a compassionate heart toward the pain of others. When I suffer, I remind myself that my suffering carries a gift within its hardship, a goal within its trial. Choosing to recognize the powerful good within my adversity, I bless all seasons of my life for their wealth and value.

Why are you so enchanted by this world when
a mine of gold lies within you?

RUMI

C&

MY CREATIVITY FUNDS
THE CREATIVITY OF ALL

My creativity is an act of my soul. I am rooted in the creativity of the entire universe. My dreams and desires are funded by divine power, intended to bring divine good and harmony into the world. As I lovingly act in the direction of my dreams, I help manifest the dreams and desires of those whom I meet along the way. My dreams prosper and encourage the dreams of others. There is no competition, no devaluing of others to reach my goals. As I flower creatively, I give to others the gift of my example. As I become larger and more magnificent,

I am a show of the power of Spirit to make all of us fuller and more abundant. There is in me only goodness, only grace. My creative dreams are blessings for the world. As I bless others through my art and artfulness, others are encouraged to flower in return. We are a garden growing into glory. I am a bloom whose glory brings beauty to all. My dreams are important to the unfolding of the world.

It is all hosannah.
It is all prayer.
Jerusalem is walking in this world.
Jerusalem is walking in this world.

THIS WORLD IS MAGICAL
IN ITS DIVERSITY, ABUNDANT
IN ITS BLESSINGS

My abundance comes to me in many forms. My life is abundant in multiple ways. I savor its specific abundance. I cherish its particular multiplicity. Loving humor, a tender smile, a compassionate conversation—all of these are forms of my abundance. Beauty in nature, the bounty of good food, music, the delight of sunlight on the skin—this is my abundance. The scent of flowers, the smell of newly mown grass—this is my abundance. The smile of a stranger, the leap of a cat, the sound of bells—this is my abundance. The satisfaction of a job well done, the pay for services rendered, the thank-you of gratitude—this, too, is my abundance. I recognize and enumerate life's generous gifts and hold them as blessings in my heart.

You are the comfort of my soul in the season of sorrow.
You are the wealth of my spirit in the heartbreak of loss.

RUMI

I AM HELD IN COMPASSIONATE ARMS

The universe is tender toward my heart. I count this a great blessing and I trust it. Frightened, threatened, or overwhelmed, I place my emotional safety in the hands of a loving universe. I ask for protection, wisdom, and discernment. Knowing that I am cared for and protected, I am alert for support and security coming to me from many directions. I find supportive people, comforting events, unexpected and gracious encounters. The world is not a hostile place. I am aided and safe. The world is my home. I am aided, safe, and protected.

True life is lived when tiny changes occur.

LEO TOLSTOY

I AM ALERT TO MY BLESSINGS

I open my eyes, ears, and heart to the goodness all around me. Rather than focus on grandiose moments of dramatic change, I focus instead on the slight, steady, constant flow of improvement in my life. In every circumstance, in each encounter, I tabulate a small, hidden blessing. I allow God to guide me into new eyes, clearer vision, the insight necessary to count and encounter my abundance. My desire to see my abundant blessings gives me eyes to see. My desire to hear my blessings gives me ears to hear. The desire of my heart to encounter and explore my blessings opens my inner horizons to depths and heights which are expansive, inspiring, and beautiful. I bless the alert attention which connects me to this world.

The present moment is filled with joy and happiness.
If you are attentive, you will see it.

THICH NHAT HANH

BLESSINGS BUILD
UPON BLESSINGS

I choose to see and build upon the good of every moment. In counting my blessings, I consciously and concretely build a life of gratitude. A life of gratitude is a life built upon optimism, expectation, and attention to the good of every instant as it unfolds. This is not denial of adversity. Rather, the choice to consciously count—and encounter—my moment-to-moment good is a spiritual discipline. My trained optimism creates in me a stamina funded in the constant flow of minute but perceptible spiritual nutrients which fuel me, body and soul. I bless my conscious attention to good.

My crippled poetry began to dance
with the light of God's Name.
His Name brought the angel of words
into the house of my mind.

RUMI

THE GREAT CREATOR
CREATES THROUGH ME

My heart is a wellspring of creative ideas. I acknowledge the blessing of my abundant inner life. Sourced—and resourced—by spirit, I am a Source of healing and inspiration for myself and others. As I reach within me in a spirit of exploration and expansion, I feel my inner horizon enlarge as I recognize larger and better possibilities for myself and for the world. When I turn to myself and my inner promptings with kind attention, I find I have many ideas and inspirations about what I can do to improve the quality of life for myself and for others. I turn with delight and anticipation to my own Inner Voice. I listen with care to its whispered suggestions. I act on the Guidance I receive and my actions, concrete and well intentioned, alter the quality of the life I lead and the life that others lead with me. My inner life blesses my outer world.

Listen to your own Self.
If you listen to that Self within, then you find the Truth.

KABIR

I ACCEPT MY BLESSINGS AS THEY UNFOLD WITHIN ME

I am blossoming in Spirit's time. Knowing this, I turn to my inner flowering securely. Within the environment of my own heart, I enjoy the sunlight of safety, the warmth of harmony, the strength of right companions. Focused on the reality that Spirit is my constant companion, I remember to be comforted by the continuity of my blessings. Grounded in the safety of divine presence, I am able to breathe deeply, pause in my striving, and notice the unfolding of one gift into another. My life is evolutionary and revolutionary. My attitude of openness, expectation, and observation yields me a sense of abundance.

Love is not a possession. It is the flow of God's energy.

SWAMI CHIDVILASANANDA

⌘

FAITH MOVES ME
TO RIGHT ACTION

I see life as a series of choices. This recognition blesses me with active faith. I choose to make my choices positive and life affirming. In the face of depression and a sense of despair, I find a small action which I can undertake toward the positive. Recognizing that my life is a matter both of proportion and perception, I work consciously to keep gratitude as my chosen attitude and optimism as the lens through which I view the world. This is not denial. This is courage. Rather than surrender to feelings of negativity and despair, I consciously and creatively combat such feelings by moving in the direction of greater faith. Rather than rehearse catastrophe, I use my thinking to remember the ever-present potential for happiness and health. I take my cue from the resilience of life itself.

The wren is small but active in the face of threatening odds. So too I choose to take personal and positive actions in the face of planetary negativity. Rather than wallow in hopelessness, I enact the viability of hope. I reach out to others with kindness and humor. I allow others to reach toward me bearing their gifts of love and healing. Rather than isolate, I communicate. I signal the world that I am engaged, committed, and active for the greater good. My active faith blesses all.

The infinite richness of the Father is mine to enjoy. The vital
good health, the wisdom, the peace, and all the good things
which proceed from the Father I now claim. The act
of accepting them is my right and privilege and I
exercise it intelligently and in full faith.

Life now sings through me in radiant ecstasy.

ERNEST HOLMES

I AM A CHILD OF DIVINE ABUNDANCE

It is my father's pleasure to give me the kingdom."
By opening our hearts to receive from the universe,
we achieve our proper position in relation to spiritual law. Spirit intends to flow to us and through us.
We are intended to allow this flow. Focusing on the
tiny increments of good which come to us daily, we
count our blessings. Counting every blessing as a small

step in the direction of my dreams, I gradually perceive my life as a safe and protected path leading in the direction of my dreams. Every time we recognize a blessing, we increase our capacity to receive a blessing. As we expand our consciousness in gratitude, we become larger vessels for good. I consciously and creatively choose to count and encounter my good. I consciously and creatively choose to expand.

Show love to all creatures and you will be happy;
for when you love all things, you love the Lord,
for He is all in all.

TULSIDAS

I AM A TRUE NOTE IN THE SYMPHONY OF LIFE

The pace of the universe brings harmony to my soul. My heart opens to the divine timing which best serves my soul. My heart paces itself according to divine unfolding. I accept and appreciate the pacing of my life. I recognize that as I seek to align myself with higher wisdom, my path is led perfectly, a step at a time, for my own highest unfolding. Spirit is the Great Conductor. I am given my cues. There is no need for haste. There is no place in me for impatience. Delays and detours to my limited vision are actually the perfect path unfolding to a higher eye. Knowing that divine timing is perfect and that I am a divinely loved child of the universe, I surrender my anxiety and urgency. I allow higher forces to orchestrate the good which is mine to have.

There is a place where words are born of silence,
A place where the whispers of the heart arise.

RUMI

I AM DIVINELY PARTNERED AND LED

I am blessed by the guidance of Spirit in many forms. I open my heart and my mind to the influence of higher forces. I relinquish my definition of myself as small and limited. I invite guidance and inspiration. I welcome new thoughts and perceptions, larger perspectives and possibilities. Rather than insist on being the sole author of my life, I invite the collaborative forces of the universe. Synchronicity, co-incidence, reinforcement, and serendipity—these are friendly companions which speak to me clearly of higher realms. Rather than close my mind to the possibility of active spiritual intervention in my affairs, I commit to noticing, noting, and acknowledging the support which I actually receive. Life is an orchestra. I am at once a musician, a music, a conductor, a composer, and an audience. I recognize my multiple roles and I embrace the harmonics of my accompaniment. I am perfectly, intricately partnered. I count this partnership a central blessing in my life.

Stand up and play the melody,
I am God.

RUMI

MY HEART KNOWS
ITS TRUE NAME

Divinity is my true nature. I am a soul among souls. I intersect those people whom I am meant to meet. Our paths cross by divine providence, not by chance or misdirection. We are blessed in our connection. Knowing this, I encounter all I meet with curiosity and gracious hospitality. I open my heart to receive them and I open my mind to acknowledge the insights and information which they bear. In every encounter, I respond and react from a position of curiosity and kinship. My heart is not closed. My heart is not defended. I am an equal among equals, a learner among learners, a friend among friends. As I seek, I too am sought. I am drawn to the people who best companion me. The people I best companion are drawn to me. My heart is secure in its divine origin. Resting in that security, I meet all souls with the recognition of their godhood, their divine spark, their dignity. Extending myself in compassion and companionship, I journey through the world with a tender and a welcoming heart. I bless this world and it blesses me in return.

When we are really honest with ourselves we must admit our lives are all that really belong to us. So it is how we use our lives that determines the kind of men we are.

CESAR CHAVEZ

THE WORLD IS BOUNTIFUL ENOUGH FOR ALL ITS CHILDREN

The world is abundant. There is enough for all of us. This is the great truth and blessing. I do not need to hoard. I do not need to grab for more. My good coexists with the good of others. What is best for me and what is best for all are one and the same. I open my heart to the highest outcome. I open my heart to the universal good. My blessings come to me freely. I do not need to compete for them. My blessings bless others as well. There is abundance for all, a right place for all. I open my heart to divine guidance in finding my right place.

To work with God-power you must give it right-of-way
and still the reasoning mind. The instant you ask,
Infinite Intelligence knows the way of fulfillment. Man's part
is to rejoice and give thanks, and act his Faith.

FLORENCE SCOVEL SHINN

THE WORLD BEFRIENDS ME

The world befriends me. In times of pain and loneliness, I ask God to open my eyes to the companionship found in the natural world. I ask to see beauty, feel grace, and know that I am partnered at all times, in all ways, by the million hands the universe sends to guide and accompany me on my travels. While I may long for contact with one special person, I ask to see the specialness in all whom I meet. I ask to be a light and a comfort to those whom I encounter. Even when troubled by loneliness, I take time to extend myself to others. Blessing the world which befriends me, I befriend the world.

In necessary things, unity; in disputed things, liberty;
in all things, charity.

RICHARD BAXTER

⌘

CHARITY GRACES MY VIEW
OF THE WORLD

M ine is a charitable heart. It is rooted in the wisdom of compassion. It is fed by the springs of self-love. Taking a compassion-ate view of myself and others, I act in the world with gentle temperance. I am not rash in action, harsh in judgment, quick in condemnation of those I see. My heart is a peaceable kingdom. Love rules its territory. Love shapes its laws.

I bless my personal charity and I choose it. My charity is born not of denial but of respect. I con-sciously choose to view all beings as having both dig-nity in their current selves and the potential to be ever more beautiful as they expand those selves. This being the case, when people grieve or disappoint me, I remind myself that the seeds of future greatness still lie within them and that my forgiving grace may be exactly the support which they need.

My charity makes me a willing servant but not a doormat. As kind as I am to others, I practice being kinder still to myself. Remembering that each of us carries the flame of divinity, I bless that flame in myself, husband its light, and then extend its charitable glow to others.

It is within my power either to serve God or not to serve him. Serving him, I add to my own good and the good of the whole world. Not serving him, I forfeit my own good and deprive the world of that good, which was in my power to create.

LEO TOLSTOY

SERVING THE WHOLE, I FEEL MYSELF TO BE A CHERISHED PART

In every moment, I am given opportunities for creative service. Sometimes that service is simple witness: I count and encounter the blessings of life. I recognize and honor the dignity of those whom I meet. Other times, the service is more heartfelt: I reach within myself to console and comfort those who are suffering and in need. There is one substance flowing through all. That substance is love. As I choose to align myself in service to its nature and my own, I also serve by example. This service is not thankless martyrdom. Loving service is an act of enlightened self-love. As I focus on others, my own troubles and losses fall into perspective. Acknowledging the worth of those I encounter, I recognize my own worth. Seeking to serve, I serve myself by experiencing the truth of my loving and expansive nature. This self-knowledge is a great blessing.

Do not weep; do not wax indignant. Understand.

BARUCH SPINOZA

KINDNESS IS MY NATURE
AND MY GIFT

My heart is a deep lake of loving-kindness. I count myself fortunate to hold tenderness within my soul. I forgive myself my fears, frailties, and failures. I am compassionate toward myself in times of turbulence and change. I remind myself that I am a gentle soul and that I have need of cherishing. I treat myself as I wish others would treat me. I treat others as they wish to be treated. I allow myself, in times of difficult and demanding strife, that I am loved and lovable, that I am worthy and respected. I do not allow temporary anxiety to distort my view of the whole. I gently seek the blessings in all difficulty while I am compassionate to myself for my lingering doubts and fears. I remind myself that my life is in the care of God and that it is unfolding with beauty and harmony.

I saw my Lord with the eye of my heart, and I said:
Who art Thou? He said: Thou.

AL-HALLAJ

☙

I KNOW MY TRUE NAME

I am a divine child and I delight in my companionship. I love myself. I enjoy my own company. I take delight in my interests, my diversions, my pastimes. I approve of myself. I honor my choices. I seek and I find integrity within my soul. I am comforted by my own companionship. I am a friend to myself. I encounter my thoughts and emotions tenderly and with interest. I have patience with myself. I do not expect too much. I am not harsh or critical. With warm support and affection I encourage my own unfolding. I trust myself to have intimacy with my own needs, wants, and dreams. I respond appropriately to my yearnings, acting ethically and forthrightly for my own best interests.

A sheltered life can be a daring life as well.
For all serious daring starts from within.

EUDORA WELTY

THE UNIVERSE GIFTS ME
WITH COURAGE
IN ALL THINGS

I cherish my own courage. I salute myself for the brave action I undertake in my life. I focus with clarity and appreciation on the choices I have made which have required courage and self-determination. I applaud myself for my strength and my daring. Rather than belittle myself for my fears, I choose to honor myself for the bravery with which I have often walked through my fears. I count back in specific ways and enumerate for myself examples of my own courage: the new friendship I have undertaken, the steadiness I have shown in a difficult job, the honesty I have displayed in opening a difficult conversation. I honor myself for my bigheartedness in the face of challenges from which I could have—but did not—shrunk back. My courage brings blessings to my life. My courage blesses the lives of others.

*Very often people don't so much doubt their guidance as their
ability to follow it. This is where friends, the right kind
of friends, come in. "Trust yourself," these friends say.
"Try it and see what happens.
Maybe your guidance is right."*

SONIA CHOQUETTE

⚬

FRIENDSHIP BLESSES
AND FULFILLS ME

I cherish the committed friendship of those who
have extended themselves on my behalf. I count
myself lucky to have the support and encourage-
ment of my friends. Rather than focus on the lacks in
my friendships, I turn my perception instead to appre-
ciating the many ways in which my friends have been
loyal and even courageous in relationship to me. I enumerate for myself the times that I have felt a friend's

courage in speaking a difficult truth. I count with gratitude the times friends have listened to me as I struggled to clarify an issue which was difficult for me to face. Rather than look at the ways in which I feel I have been let down or betrayed, I choose today to focus on the ways in which I have been nurtured, encouraged, and protected.

THE UNIVERSE TEACHES ME
WITH GENTLE LOVE

Spirit mentors me with care and accuracy. As I open my heart and my hand to be counseled, I am partnered by divine wisdom. It is a great blessing that I do not walk alone. I am not without guidance. In every day, in every moment, there is a source of divine guidance available to me if I will turn within. Within me, I carry God. Within God, I am carried. There is no separation, only the forgetting of union. As I realize, accept, and appreciate my union with divinity, all things unfold for me more clearly. As

I accept the grace within my current circumstances, my grace increases and flows forward to prepare my future. My life is a life of abundant blessings. My heart is a home for grace and good. As I cherish the gifts which accompany me now, I see greater gifts, greater love still unfolding. As I open my eyes to see and my ears to hear, I find the beauty of life is dazzling. This green planet, this garden, returns to grace as I am guided to husband it as carefully as I would my child. Graced and protected by higher forces, acutely attuned to higher goods, I protect and shepherd this planet to deepened health. My guidance blesses me and all I touch.

The truth is that this world is full of love. This world is an embodiment of the bliss of God. Look at the trees— God's love is vibrating in them. Look at the water— God's love is vibrating in water. Look at the faces of all the people—God's love is vibrating there.

SWAMI MUKTANANDA

MY LIFE IS A TREASURE CHEST AND I COUNT ITS WORTH

The life which I have now is rich and beautiful, intricate and valuable. I cherish the abundance which has come to my door. I take the time and attention to focus on the precise components of my life which please me. I notice the beauty of my surroundings, the harmony of my friendships, the synergy of the many parts working together to form a greater whole. I survey the life that I have created with fondness. I pause and appreciate the many small gifts which have brought me delight and renewal. Through the act of consciously cherishing what I do have, I open the doorway to even greater abundance. Allowing the changes in my life to build one upon the other, I allow a transformation in my needs and wants to coexist with appreciation for what I have wanted and have loved. Life is an evolutionary process. Each larger form is built upon the form from which it moves beyond. Recognizing this, I hold tenderness in my heart for both my past and my present. I allow my future to unfold, organically rooted in the soil of all I have been. I bless the treasure of my own unfolding.

What is really yours? The blessings you bring to yourself, through your spoken or silent word; the things you see with your inner eye.

FLORENCE SCOVEL SHINN

I GROW WITH NATURAL GRACE

I cherish the pace which God provides for my growth. I accept the tempo of God's action as appropriate to my native interests. Taking my cue from the seasons, I count my blessings in the small daily events which mark my calendar. What one small thing did I notice today that was filled with beauty? What small thing did I do today which expressed love? Rather than seeking always to have a life flooded by abundance, I turn to cherishing what I do have and husbanding it with care and gratitude. Rather than focusing on what more I would like to have, I focus on what I can do better to honor and respect that which I do have. I cherish my precise point of growth.

Go confidently in the direction of your dreams! Live the life you've imagined. As you simplify your life, the laws of the universe will be simpler.

HENRY DAVID THOREAU

⌘

I AM THE DREAM OF GOD
DREAMING GOD

I am a dreamer of divine dreams. The dreams of my heart are dreams which God fulfills for me. As I yearn, my prayer is heard and the answer is prepared. My every thought, my every action, is a moment in which divine support comes to me. I am never alone, never an exile, never a stranger from the heart of God. The heart of God holds me within its bountiful soil. I blossom there, rooted in faith, fed by the nutrients of divine love. As I source myself in God, as I draw my strength from divine abundance, divine supply, there is no lack, no shortcoming. Apparent delays and denials are truly detours which route me toward a higher good. I allow divine wisdom to alter and expand the dreams of my heart. I accept divine guidance, divine wisdom, and divine fulfillment. My dreams are good and goodness is the nature of God. My dreams, therefore, are God's. I go to God for their fulfillment.

We are scraps of iron. Your love is the magnet
that draws us near.

RUMI

I AM A PARTICLE OF GOD
AND AN ARTICLE OF FAITH
IN ACTION

My destiny is unique and irreplaceable. My gifts and perceptions are powerful and important. My needs, goals, and desires are an outer manifestation of my inner divinity seeking to express itself for the good of all. As I realize my dreams I am an example to others that their dreams, too, have weight and consequence. As I harbor myself gently and birth my dreams carefully, I show by the respect with which I treat myself the respect with which all of us deserve to be treated. In acting toward myself in concrete and loving ways, I become ever more able to love others consciously and concretely. As I allow myself to receive good from my own hand, I also open myself to receiving good from others, giving them the gift of knowing that their love and contributions are felt by me as honored and important parts of my life. As I cherish myself, I cherish others as well. I am ever more loving, ever more heart-centered as I recognize that each of us desires and deserves a tender love which encourages us toward expansion. My active faith in the unique destiny of each of us blesses all I encounter with the gift of being truly, fully seen.

There are two aspects of individual harmony; the harmony
between body and soul, and the harmony between individuals.

HAZRAT INAYAT KHAN

MY FRIENDSHIPS ARE
A BEAUTIFUL HARVEST

I cherish the companions Spirit has given me. I honor those who share my life. I bless their talents, abilities, gifts, and personalities. I see them as divinely led, divinely placed in connection to me and to our mutual unfolding. Calling to mind that divinity resides within each of us, I regard all my relationships as sacred interactions, opportunities to experience Spirit in human form. Recognizing this, I draw on my own inner divinity to act with dignity and kindness, with harmony and grace. The spirit of universal love moves through me, to me, and out from me in all my connections. In every relationship, the heart of Spirit fills my heart with loving grace. I count my friendships as valued jewels. The hearts of my friends are my diamonds, emeralds, rubies, sapphires, and pearls. The unique gems of their personalities are their own divine spark. I cherish each for its beauty and richness.

*The truth is that the inner Self of every human being is
supremely great and supremely lovable. Everything is
contained in the Self. The divine Principle that
creates and sustains this world pulsates within us
as our own Self. It scintillates in the heart and
shines through all our senses.*

SWAMI MUKTANANDA

ALL OF HUMANITY IS
MY BELOVED FAMILY

We are one tribe. I cherish our unity. We are
united by our suffering and by our joy.
One life flows through all life. One heart
holds every heart. The loss I sustain today is the beginning of a larger, wiser, and kinder tomorrow. It is a
part of the dignity of those we lose that we go forward
bearing them as loving treasure in our hearts. I cherish

those whom I carry in my heart. I honor their thoughts, their wisdom, their guidance, and their support. I bring them forward through my actions toward the future they empowered.

Every branch and leaf and fruit
reveals some aspect of God's
perfection: the cypress gives hint
of His majesty; the rose gives
tidings of His beauty.

JAMI

I AM ONE WITH ALL THERE IS

I am connected to all of life. All of life blesses me with its connection. Even as I am able to value the beauty of a crystal, the radiance of a lily, the delicacy of a fern, so too am I beautiful and to be valued. As strong as an oak, as enduring in value as a rock formation, as intricate and individual as a snowflake, I am as consciously and as carefully created and crafted as any of these. Furthermore, I carry within me the co-creative powers to add to my beauty and my worth. As I chose to contribute to life, as I choose to consciously and creatively live to my fullest flowering, I become an expansion of the creator within me. This blesses all.

The Divine Spirit is flowing through me in an individual
way and I accept the genius of my own being.

ERNEST HOLMES

☙

I VOICE THE UNIVERSE
IN AN ORIGINAL WAY

I bring to life a unique and powerful voice. My insights and perceptions are important blessings. Voicing my insights and perceptions is important to the world. I am an irreplaceable individual whose gifts benefit all. Owning my gifts, inhabiting them, and expanding them are my gifts to the world and those with whom I share it. As I become larger, more color-ful, and more truly myself, I create for others the real-ization that it is safe for them to become larger, more vibrant, more fully alive. Moving upward and outward in a spirit of creative community, I am non-competitive and truly collaborative, growing larger myself while helping others to achieve their true size as well. The cosmic web is alive with greater and greater consciousness, larger and brighter possibility. As I extend my hand in my immediate world, I alter and enlarge the benevolence of the world as a whole. My every action is sweet and significant. Knowing this, I consciously and creatively act for the highest good. My unique voice and consciousness bless all.

We can smile, breathe, walk, and eat our meals in a way that allows us to be in touch with the abundance of happiness that is available. We are very good at preparing to live, but not very good at living.

THICH NHAT HANH

MY HEART IS A GATEWAY FOR BLESSINGS TO UNFOLD

I celebrate the present abundance of my life. I enumerate and enjoy the many blessings which I do have and those I see now entering my life. I allow myself to count over the many dreams I have which have come true. I allow myself to enjoy the gifts which are already manifested in my experience. For example, I have friends who are loyal and true, whose conversation and companionship cheer me. This is a deep blessing and one which I remember to cherish. In my home, I have objects whose beauty brings me delight whenever I gaze on them. I am able even years after the acquisition to enjoy the grace and artistry with which beautiful objects have been made. On a seasonal level, new sights and sounds fill my life with delight: birds nest, breezes stir, the scent of flowers perfumes the air. For these many blessings, I give thanks. As I bless the abundance I do enjoy, I open my heart's capacity to receive even more.

Your words create what you speak about.
Learn to speak positively.

SANAYA ROMAN

I REST IN ABUNDANT SUPPLY

There are many doors through which my abundance comes to me. I bless them all. I am careful to allow many avenues for my good to flow to me. Rather than focus on one person or event as the sole source of my opportunity, I allow the universe to source me from myriad people and events. I open myself deeply and fully to the fact that I am held and embraced by an interactive universe. I am able to trigger my good by triggering good for others. As I concentrate on positive outflow, abundant inflow comes to me. I am sustained. I am expanded. I am prospered and blessed.

I create my own security by trusting the process of life.

LOUISE L. HAY

I AM SAFE AND SECURE

The heart of God holds all in safety. In times of separation from those I love, I remind myself that all of us are held safely in the heart of God. I ask God to touch those I love with healing grace and compassion. I ask God to gently guide those I love to their highest good and sweetest outcomes. While I long for physical contact with those I love, I remind myself that we are always in touch in spirit and that I touch them directly with grace whenever I pray for their happiness and well-being. Asking God to act for me, I pray for abundant blessings to those I love.

I BLOOM
IN THE GARDEN
OF GOD

God is the divine gardener and all souls bloom in divine love. As a green shoot welcomes the sun, I welcome the gardening hand of God. All souls are equal. All souls are rooted in God's soil. I am both a gardener and a flower blooming in the field of God. As a gardener, I ask that my hands be capable and gentle. I ask that I bring to the world beauty and tenderness, love and appreciation. As a part of the very garden which I tend, I ask that I flower fully, showing myself in my greatest beauty. I ask that I unfold perfectly, that my nature be a delight to those around me. Knowing my need for nutrients and care, I allow myself to be nurtured, shaped, and sheltered by those who care for me. In the blossoming of humankind, I gladly take my place as both a beauty and a caretaker of beauty. Humbled by the glory of the natural world, I bless the garden which contains us all.

I learned that the real creator was my inner Self,
the Shakti. . . . That desire to do something
is God inside talking through us.

MICHELE SHEA

MY HEART IS HOME TO PEACEFUL EXPANSION

I am a field resting in the sun. My dreams germinate and grow within the security of divine love. Grace dreams with me and through me. All of my dreams are divine in origin. All of my dreams are divinely fulfilled. As I reside in grace and grace resides in me, my endeavors are shaped and secured by the action of loving grace in the world. As I honor the promptings of my heart, I honor the heart of the universe. My wishes, goals, and desires are divinely sheltered, divinely inspired, divinely protected. Resting in divine power, they are harmonious in their unfolding; their unfolding is pivotal to the working-out of the greater good. Secure in universal power, my dreams and passions find powerful pathways to manifestation as grace births them to prosper in this world. I am peace expanding.

*Our vision is beclouded and the pathway of our progress is
obstructed until we come to know that God can and does
express as Good in every person and situation.*

ERNEST HOLMES

I WALK IN PEACE

I walk in peace. Adversity melts away as I remember the spiritual reality underlying all things. I claim my right to divine comfort, divine harmony. I release all apparent discord into the healing care of the universe, trusting completely in the larger good that is unfolding. Divine calm centers my heart in its loving presence. I relax. Remembering I am sourced in divine protection, I breathe in contentment and well-being. I am held in the heart of God. All things work toward the good. As I embrace my part in a larger and holier whole, that whole embraces me. This unity is a great blessing which brings peace and comfort to my heart.

O rich and various man! Thou palace of sight and sound,
carrying in thy senses the morning and the night, and the
unfathomable galaxy; in thy brain, the geometry of the city
of God; in thy heart, the power of love.

RALPH WALDO EMERSON

I AM IN THE CENTER
OF GOD'S LOVE

The heart of God knows no distance. I am held and cherished in the heart of God. I am safe, protected, and companioned at all times. There is no place or circumstance in which I am alone, without divine company and counsel. In times of loneliness, I remind myself that God infuses all things: the chair, the table, the rug, the flower, the vase. Divinity flows through all life and is all life. My fingertips contain God. God is at my fingertips at all times. When I feel loneliness, fatigue, or despair, I comfort myself by knowing I am contained within the heart of God and if I will only look for God within my own heart, I will find both of us there.

Just remain in the center, watching.
And then forget that you are there.

L A O - T Z U

I AM IMMERSED
IN DIVINE LIFE

The river of God flows through my experience. My life is sourced in universal life. My gifts come to me from Spirit. Drawing upon Spirit, I live my life fully and joyously. I encounter difficulty with resiliency. I encounter adversity with faith. Sourced in Spirit, gifted by Spirit, I am enough, more than enough, for any calamity. Rooted in Spirit, my soul is wealthy. Help and companions come to me in troubled times. I draw upon Spirit as I would a deep, clear, and pure stream of healing water. Dipping my heart into the flow of faith, I emerge refreshed and energized despite the severity of the hardships which I encounter. Spirit blesses my life.

If anything is sacred, the human body is sacred.

WALT WHITMAN

⌒

MY HEALTH IS ROOTED
IN GOD

I honor the physical gift of health with which God has graced me. I give thanks for my vitality, my clarity, my vibrancy. Drawing strength from my connection to the natural world, I allow the physical vehicle of my body to be cherished and loved. Rather than focusing on what I wish were different, I focus instead on the loving loyalty and service which my body has so freely given me. Rather than say, "I wish this part of me were different," I instead say, "I am grateful that this part of me is exactly as it is." There is at least one feature of mine which I can wholly cherish: my eyes, my nose, my hair, my hands, feet, or shoulders. Today I willingly and positively focus on the beauty of the physical form which I have been given.

*Our physical body possesses a wisdom which we who inhabit
the body lack. We give it orders which make no sense.*

HENRY MILLER

MY BODY IS MY TEACHER
AND MY GUIDE

My body is more than a vehicle which carries me through life. My body is a storehouse for my memories, a sensitive radar kit which warns me of danger, a wise teacher who signals me how best to care for my spirit. When I listen to my body, I am led into right and wise actions. When I take seriously the guidance it offers, I make decisions which honor me in a holistic way.

My body grounds me and protects me. My body is sacred and as knowing as a temple oracle. Often the intuitive warnings of my body regarding people, places, and events are the deepest safety I am given. I bless my body for its loyal surveillance on my behalf. I bless my body for its patient endurance, its mercurial intuition, and its persistence in speaking to me even when I slough aside the guidance it bears. My body is the most loyal of my friends. I bless my body for its loyal companionship and commit to regarding it with tender care.

MY LIFE IS VALUABLE
AND INTERESTING

I value my sense of history. I am alert to the many colorful and enjoyable episodes in my own life's unfolding. Rather than bemoan a lack of color or adventure in my life, I consciously choose to notice and appreciate the many small adventures and victories which each of my days entertains. I focus on the precise and measurable evidence of good that comes to me as I am alert to life's many blessings. I notice, remark, and remember the kind word, the well-told joke, the flashing beauty of a small finch lighting on a roadside shrub. Alert to the beauty and detail around me, I revel ever more fully in the many graces life has to offer me.

Prayer is an attitude of the heart.

LARRY DOSSEY

MY HEART BRIMS WITH AFFECTION AND EXPANSION

I am committed to gratitude in my life. This choice opens my perceptions to receive my good. This choice shows me the inner doorway through which abundance comes to me. My heart is connected to universal love. Opening to my inner connection to Source, I receive an inflow of love and further gratitude. I give out an outflow of love and further gratitude. Gratitude for me is active. It is an inner decision to name and cherish what I love. It is a recognition of the many ways in which I myself am loved and cherished. In committed gratitude, I strive to touch all with the loving-kindness which touches me. I practice the principles of love in action. I am kind and compassionate first to myself and then to all others. I cherish our worth, our dignity, our shared path as co-creative beings shaping our shared world.

My heart holds within it every form,
it contains a pasture for gazelles,
a monastery for Christian monks.

IBN ARABI

I CELEBRATE THE UNITY
OF ALL LIFE

One life runs through everything. The oak, the elm, the ash, my own body, the dove, the doe, the ox—all are creatures of one life. Rooted in this knowledge, I live carefully and consciously. I bless all creatures and all elements of this earth. I live in harmony. I live with grace. I walk humbly and in friendship with all that lives. I open my heart to the teachings of all of life. I learn from water, from soil, from budding growth. I learn from harvest, from decline, and from decay. I embrace the cycles of the living world. I take my place on the wheel of life. I lead and I follow. I partner and am partnered. I accept the grace and companionship of all with whom I share this earth. I bless the unity of life.

Because he believes in himself,
he doesn't try to convince others.
Because he is content with himself,
he doesn't need others' approval.
Because he accepts himself,
the whole world accepts him.

TAO-TE CHING

MY SOUL IS
A DIVINE COMPANION

I count myself fortunate to be my own companion on life's journey. I am interested by my thoughts and perceptions. I am conscious of the many gifts I bring to living: my stamina, my humor, my perceptivity, my integrity. I count myself lucky to be responsible for my unfolding. I appreciate my commitment to being personally responsible for the caliber of my life, for undertaking an active role in the quality of my own life. I applaud my ability to act decisively on my own behalf, to seek out persons and activities which are of interest to me. I remind myself that I am lucky indeed to have someone of my own caliber as my constant friend, my loyal ally. Rather than berate myself for shortcomings or imagined flaws, I cherish the many parts of my character which make me a pleasure in my own life.

Let your heart's light guide you to my house.
Let your heart's light show you that we are one.

RUMI

⁂

LOYALTY IS MY GIFT
AND MY LANTERN

I esteem myself for my loyalty. I recognize that my capacity to commit and continue in relationships has been an invaluable part of what has brought richness and continuity to my life. I commend myself for the willingness I have displayed to work through differences with those I love. I honor myself for my stamina in challenging emotional situations. I appreciate my ability to allow differences to be aired, recognized, and worked through. I value my capacity for undertaking the responsibility of long-term relationships. I salute the part of me which has the maturity and compassion to allow myself and others to expand and evolve. I bless my lantern-heart and allow it to light my path.

*You must remember that man is noble, man is sublime, man
is divine, and can accomplish whatever he desires.*

SWAMI MUKTANANDA

MY STRENGTH IS A FORTRESS

I cherish the depths of my inner resources. I have far more stamina, resiliency, and power than I sometimes know. Counting my true reservoirs of inner potency, I see that I am strong—stronger than I know, even stronger than I need. Every power that I need to meet my life is a power which is already contained within me. I am funded in universal strength. Claiming that power to be my bedrock and my birthright, I meet adversity with calm fortitude. I bless my strength. I bless the security that it provides.

*I realize there is a Divine Presence at the center of my
being. I let this recognition flow down into the
very depths of my being. Every thought and condition
contrary to the Divine Perfection is eliminated.
I rejoice in this realization.*

ERNEST HOLMES

I WALK IN SPIRITUAL BEAUTY

Divine presence is the foundation of my life. It is solid and unshakable. It is permanent, eternal, and always present. I am the recipient of great goodwill. This goodwill is timeless and unchanging. There is a benevolent force which intends me good and expansion. I receive blessings from many quarters. My good comes to me from all directions and at all times. I rest in divine love as my fortress. I am surrounded by good. Good upholds me and is my strength. In all my endeavors, in all my affairs, good unfolds and prospers me. Good blesses all of my relationships. My spirit and my life are one with the benevolent force of the universe.

DIVINE GUIDANCE SPEAKS
WITHIN ME AND
THROUGH THE WORLD

Divine love guides me. I count—and I count on—this blessing. Reminding myself that Spirit always speaks both to me and through me, I listen with my heart and I hear with clarity. In every situation, I find the path of compassion, the voice of higher wisdom. I am able to hear divine guidance. I seek my inner wisdom and it comes to me. It is always there. There is a right solution, a good outcome for every difficulty. The world evolves in all its particulars toward higher good and harmony. I am able to be a part of this upward evolution as I listen and respond to my inner cues. I do not need to act out of fear. I do not need to force solutions. My inner wisdom guides me. As I listen to my heart, I find support in the outer world. There is no place too isolated for guidance to reach me through inner and outer promptings. I ask to be led. I listen within me and without. The world responds to my listening with a voice of compassion and clear guidance. I am blessed by the guidance I receive.

Life is sacred. Life is art. Life is sacred art.

GABRIELLE ROTH

CS

MY LIFE IS A JEWEL BOX
OF PRECIOUS MOMENTS

When I count and encounter my blessings, I experience a sense of fullness, safety, and satisfaction. I have enough. My heart is bountiful. My life is dowried by rich companions and rewarding experiences. As I experience the power and goodness of the universe, I experience my own power and goodness. I experience that I am enough—more than enough. I experience flow, increased flow and expanded flow. Opening to receive this flow, I become larger and more magnificent. I am part of a grand and glorious design. A grand and glorious design is part of me. I celebrate the grandeur of this fact with a humble heart.

In the garden every flower
Has its purpose and its hour—
The tulip and delphinium,
To only name a minimum.

"AVALON," JULIA CAMERON

ॐ

DIVERSITY IS RAINBOW-HUED IN MY EXPERIENCE

Mine is a multicolored life. It is rich in its differences, rewarding in its rich and variable components. My friendships, my interests, travels, and my pursuits bring me a world of variety, a wealth of differing goods. While grounded in my individual life, I am privileged to share the colorful lives of many. My explorations culturally, intellectually, and spiritually bring to me the riches from many horizons, the bounty of many lands. I embrace diversity in my life. I accept it, invite it, and enjoy it.

We know how to sacrifice ten years for a diploma, and we are willing to work very hard to get a job, a car, a house, and so on. But we have difficulty remembering that we are alive in the present moment, the only moment there is for us to be alive. Every breath we take, every step we make, can be filled with peace, joy, and serenity. We need only to be awake, alive in the present moment.

THICH NHAT HANH

I WELCOME JOY AS MY SPIRITUAL COMPANION

I invite joy to bless my life. I welcome joy to my heart. Asceticism, hardship, grandiosity—these are enemies, not the handmaidens of spiritual growth. Gentleness, opening attention—these are the gardening tools which best encourage growth. In every moment, I can choose between will and willingness, between determination and fructification. As I allow myself to be rendered gently fruitful, I become fluid from moment to moment. The harshness of my experience slips away. Spirituality requires vulnerability and openness. As I still myself rather than "steel" myself, I hear ever more clearly the quiet promptings of inner growth. As I follow the lead which joy sets in my life, I am gently, safely, and surely led.

*We are told that prayer brings angels down. But if prayer is
thought, concentrated and distilled, the clear, pure yearning
of the heart, is prayer itself also the manifestation of
the divine? The desire itself being granted as a gift of God,
in order that its satisfaction may be given us by God?*

SOPHY BURNHAM

I AM SECURE IN THE FLOW
OF GRACEFUL GOOD

I anticipate the blessings hidden in all circumstances. Therefore, I surrender my need to control
relationships and events. I open my heart to divine
outcomes, divine timing. I allow my agendas to become divine agendas. I allow the forms and functions
of people and situations to unfold naturally to the
highest good. Guided by grace and guarded by grace,
the people and circumstances of my life flow into

shapes which benefit everyone. I allow Spirit to shape my life into ever more satisfying forms. I invite Spirit to counsel me on how I can best cooperate with, rather than control, the graceful unfolding of my good.

Committed to accepting specific suggestions in all circumstances, knowing that Spirit is precise and particular, I accept the guidance of God: good, orderly direction. I surrender my resistance to the action of grace in my endeavors. I open my heart to the creative input of higher realms. I allow divine guidance to enter and act in my affairs, moving and shaping the events of my life into ever more perfect forms, ever more tangible blessings. The action of grace is concrete and substantial. As I invite the action of grace into my life, my blessings are guaranteed.

Respect is love. The heart is also love—and so are you.

MY WORLD IS FILLED
WITH GRACEFUL LOVE

My path is broad and gentle. Ours is a journey of shared hearts. I remind myself that I am blessed with friendship, gifted with acquaintances and associations who travel with me toward the highest good. Reminding myself, always, that we are all traveling together, I develop my individuality while welcoming the individuality of others. As much as I yearn to be truly seen and truly loved, I seek to see others truly and truly love them. I offer to those I encounter a believing mirror. I reflect back to them their dignity, their beauty, their potential and divine spark. Treating all whom I encounter with respect and affection, I allow my heart to be a vessel for healing love. Drawing on universal love to love through me, I love freely and without fatigue. I open my heart to actualizing grace in each encounter. I allow Spirit to enter my interactions, shaping them and leavening them to a richer bread. I am nourished by Spirit and through Spirit. I seek to bless and nourish others by expressing Spirit through me.

We should always remember:
God reveals Himself to us within us in the form of love.

SWAMI MUKTANANDA

I WITNESS THE GOOD IN OTHERS AND CELEBRATE THEIR GROWTH

The growth of one blesses all. I am committed to grow in love. All that I touch, I leave in love. I move through this world consciously and creatively. I act with quiet authority moving from my heart to touch the dreams and hearts of others. As I faithfully mirror to others their worth and their precious and irreplaceable individuality, I myself play an irreplaceable part in bringing the world to greater abundance. So often all that is needed is an act of loving attendance. I marshal myself to offer that witness.

In witnessing others in their passage I ratify the importance of my own. Life is led both individually and collectively. I honor my importance and the importance of others. None of us is dispensable, none of us is replaceable. In the chorus of life each of us brings a True Note, a perfect pitch which adds to the harmony of the whole. I act creatively and consciously to actively endorse and encourage the expansion of those whose lives I touch. Believing in the goodness of each, I add to the goodness of all. We bless each other even in passing.

New, wonderful experiences now enter my life. I am safe.

LOUISE LILTAY

I WELCOME THE ARRIVAL OF NEW LOVES

I give thanks for my new friendships. I welcome my new loves, my new acquaintances. Knowing that we have intersected as part of a higher plan, I extend my heart and my hand to new people and new events, welcoming them home to their place in my world. Rather than live in a closed, insular, and distanced manner, I fling open the doors to my heart. My life is a courtyard filled by the sun. My courtyard is peopled by those I love and those whom I am learning to love. I bless my capacity to love. My capacity to love blesses me.

It would be good to find some quiet inlet where the waters
were still enough for reflection, where one might sense
the joy of the moment, rather than plan breathlessly
for a dozen mingled treats in the future.

KATHLEEN NORRIS

MY LIFE IS A WELLSPRING OF GRACE

I am sourced in divine flow. It pours out from me, shaped by me uniquely, to bless my world. My spiritual essence matters to me and others. As I am true to myself, I am true to others. I am divinely led and guided in all my dealings. Trusting in this, I offer others the safety of honest companionship, the reality of grounded love. Drawing on God source, my love is pure and healing. It is divine water for a thirsty world. I bless the flow which flows through me. This flow blesses my world.

I AM UNIQUE
AND IRREPLACEABLE

My personality, with all its quirks, foibles, and eccentricities, is a perfect expression of God energy moving into the world. I cherish my individual expression of divine life. I acknowledge that I am uniquely designed to bring certain energies into play in an innovative and beneficial way for all. There is something in my own creative makeup that is necessary to the good of the world. I am designed specifically to make a unique and meaningful contribution. There is a beauty and a purpose to my precise personality. I am not an accident, a mistake, or a haphazard collection of influences. I am a self-evolving and important energy which brings to the world a precise and important healing medicine. My influence and impact on others is a matter of large consequence. Believing this is not a matter of ego. It is a recognition of the divine plan which embraces us all. I am a pivotal and important part of this plan. My actions and attitudes have weight and consequence. As I consciously and creatively come into my full flowering, I bring the best and the brightest of myself as blessings into the world.

Forgiveness multiplies and melts rigid postures.
Try again and again with self-forgiveness.
Be the kind parent to yourself you may not have had.

I EXPAND MY HEART
IN THE SAFETY OF
SPIRITUAL PROTECTION

I commit myself to the blessing of self-expansion. I am a part of a larger whole, but that larger whole is also a part of me. I can expand or contract my consciousness according to my openness and receptivity. As I harbor feelings of disappointment and betrayal, I block the flow of my larger good. As I clear the air by acknowledging the wounds I have allowed to dampen my faith, I enter a fuller and more firmly based relationship with my larger self. I therefore commit myself to fully facing and feeling the complicated emotions that arise within me as I move through my world. Choosing to be intimate first to myself and to God and then to others, I commit to staying current with myself and with my companions. Through this commitment, I allow life to flow through me like a river. Its flow washes me clear of debris while bearing to me the silt for richer growth. I accept the blessing of my own expansive nature.

Satisfaction of one's curiosity is one of the greatest sources of happiness in life.

LINUS PAULING

ॐ

MY MIND IS NOURISHED BY DIVINE IDEAS

I count myself lucky to have the opportunities which surround me for intellectual fulfillment. I count with delight the ways in which my life is enriched by the resources which are at hand. Rather than focus on what is lacking, I choose today to enumerate the things which do interest and delight me. I count the areas in which I have abundant resources. I am grateful for the diversity of my friends and my community. Choosing to see that I can play an increasingly accurate role in my own self-nurturance, I recognize the many as yet untapped arenas for self-enrichment with which I am supplied. It is a matter of perception whether I choose to view my life as half-filled and able to be ever more abundant or half-empty and ever more disappointing. Recognizing that the choice is mine, I turn my focus toward the ways in which I can deepen and expand my mind and my spirit. My mind is blessed by the food of my intellectual interests.

Tenacity is when you follow your heart—when the whole world is screaming to get back into your head.

SONIA CHOQUETTE

Cᛒ

MY TENACITY IS A POWERFUL ENGINE FOR GOOD

I am blessed by my own tenacity. I contain an inner reservoir of gritty strength, which serves me and others well. My capacity to stick to a commitment is a safe and trustworthy component of my character. My tenacity is the building block for my successful career, relationship, family life, and friendships.

Obstacles test me but they do not deter me. I am able, always, to tap an inner resilient strength which serves me. Even when life is a desert, I find my careful way. Like a camel, I carry within myself stamina and the wisdom to use my energy wisely for the long trek.

I am a creature of miraculous endurance. My will and my grounded passion form the basis for my tenacious movement through life. I bless my tenacity for its important, unsung heroism.

It is said that desire is a product of the will, but the converse is in fact true: will is a product of desire.

DENIS DIDEROT

♆

MY WILL IS A POWERFUL ENERGY USED FOR GOOD

I bless the steely temper of my will. The steel of my resolve graces me with tenacity, blesses me with endurance, and assures me of success. My will is a potent force which carries me in the direction of good. As I set my will on worthy objectives and goals, as I focus my will and act in accordance with its desires, I find myself moving effectively and powerfully in the world. My will is rooted in divine guidance and expressed as right action. My will is a sword that cuts away difficulties and defends the values I cherish. I bless my will for its very willingness to bless me.

*If we are not fully ourselves, truly in
the present moment, we miss everything.*

THICH NHAT HANH

☙

I LIVE IN THE POWER OF
THE MOMENT

Every moment is a power point for creative choice. This realization is a great blessing. Knowing this, I choose to live my life consciously and concretely, moment by moment, choosing attitudes and actions which cause my life to flourish and expand. I am an arrow shot through time. My consciousness carries my accumulated energy and wisdom. As I allow my fullest self to choose my thoughts and behaviors, I act creatively and expansively. My rich life becomes richer still. I am alert to inner and outer promptings which cause me to recognize and respond to my ever-increased opportunities, my ever-increased blessings. As I create for myself an inner expectation of enlarged goodness and potential, my life becomes adventurous, optimistic, and expansive. In each moment, I choose the highest good, the clearest path, the most openhearted perspective. Each choice, each moment blesses me. I count my good fortune at every turn.

Nobody sees a flower—really—it is so small it takes
time—we haven't time—and to see takes time,
like to have a friend takes time.

GEORGIA O'KEEFFE

$\mathcal{C}\hspace{-2pt}\mathcal{E}$

THE EARTH IS MY JOY
AND COMFORT

The earth consoles me in all things. In times of grief, I turn to the natural world. I allow the earth to comfort me. I study the lesson of cyclicality. I see the place of death in life. Faced with loss, I seek comfort in the heart of loss. In every loss, at its very heart, is the gift of life. When I am tempted by despair, I look more closely at the face of grief. I see its dignity, its humanity. I see that I am part of a larger whole. There is no loss which is new to this earth. There is no grief which is larger than life. The most

· 147 ·

grievous loss, the most devastating catastrophe—at its heart even this grief is embraced by a compassionate earth. I bless the heart of this green planet which cradles us all.

*Animals are in possession of themselves; their soul
is in possession of their body.*

GEORG HEGEL

⌘

THE ANIMAL KINGDOM
BLESSES MY LIFE

E ven in the midst of the city, I find daily contact
with animals that cheer me and help me to put
my life into perspective. I bless the companionship of all animals as they cross my path: the calico
cat sitting in the window above the window box of
pansies; the white dove flying with its darker sisters as
I pass the gothic hulk of a city church; the sunny
spaniel strolling at its owner's side on a city street—all
of these creatures light my heart and remind me of my
own animal nature.

Animals have the gift of living in the moment.

They inhabit their physical world with attention and grace. Taking a cue from their presence, I learn the lesson of attention, the blessing of alert focus on the world around me.

Chance is always powerful. Let your hook be always cast;
in the pool where you least expect it, there will be a fish.

O V I D

MY LIFE IS SHAPED BY DIVINE GUIDANCE TO GREATER BEAUTY

I open myself to the freedom of change. I bless the changes which come to me. Trusting in change, I relax my grip on the contours of my life. I allow new beginnings. I allow alteration, accommodation, change. I invite the interaction of imagination and possibility. I surrender agendas, outlines, plots. Recognizing that life is both active and interactive, I hold out my hand to dance, knowing that I am partnered more variably and creatively than I can yet conceive. I bless the changeable creativity of life in its unfolding.

It is not because things are difficult that we do not dare;
it is because we do not dare that they are difficult.

SENECA

With courage you will dare to take risks,
have the strength to be compassionate and the
wisdom to be humble. Courage is the
foundation of integrity.

KESHAVEN NAIR

THE UNIVERSE FUNDS ME WITH POWER AND PROTECTION

I am a power to be reckoned with. I salute my capacity to act. My choices and decisions, my attitudes and actions shape the world in which I live. Sourced in God, I have tremendous resources which I can marshal for good. As I pass through every day, my respect and receptivity to others help determine the caliber of world which we share. There is no moment in which I cannot make a positive contribution. By my choices and my concrete and personal actions, I directly impact the lives of all with whom I deal. My smile, my concerned question, my joke or gaiety, these impact not only those with whom I interact but also all those with whom they interact. My consciousness is a fountain of good. As I pour forth positive energy, I change the world. Life is made of small moments which have a large impact. My positive belief and support can help to change the trajectory of a lifetime. As I mirror to others their true value and worth, I create a world in which all of us are more truly valued. I bless with dignity all those I encounter.

Truly it is in the darkness that one finds the light, so when we are in sorrow, then this light is nearest all of us.

MEISTER ECKHART

I ACCEPT MY LOSS AS THE GATEWAY TO GAIN

The universe gives to me by what it takes away. My loss is a gain which I am as yet unable to see. As I let go of the good to which I cling, other good moves toward me. As I surrender my short-sighted agenda, events and people better suited to my long-term happiness enter my life. In the face of loss, I feel my feelings but I do not draw conclusions based on false evidence appearing real. I remind myself that life is evolutionary, that situations have a way of working toward my good if I will stand aside in faith and allow the hand of the universe to set things right. I bless the grace active in my life which carries all things toward the good.

I turn to the Presence of God at the center of my being and it is here that I discover the nature of the Good which must and does reside in the back of all people and events.

ERNEST HOLMES

ADVERSITY IS MISPERCEPTION AS ALL WORKS TOWARD THE GOOD

I bless my perceived rival. I affirm my inner worth regardless of outcome. I affirm, too, the inner worth of my perceived rival. Knowing all works together for the good, I claim for each of us the highest good. I expect the working-out of our difficulties to create the best path for each of us. Knowing that no one person can block my good, I surrender my sense of adversity. There is enough good for all. Each of us is prospered by and through each other. My perceived rival is a means to my achieving a good end. I bless my disguised friend.

In the middle of difficulty lies opportunity.

ALBERT EINSTEIN

MY HEART IS A GATEWAY
FOR GOD

My faith is a lantern in times of darkness, a gentle hearth against the cold. My response to loss is faith. My response to a door which closes is anticipation of another, more appropriate, door opening. As I release my insistence on having my good come to me from the persons and situations which I myself select, I open myself to greater good which comes to me from more persons and more sources than I can yet imagine. The universe is abundant in its desires for me. There is a plan and a perfect pace for my blossoming and unfolding. In the face of loss, I feel my feelings and I accept them. That done, I respond next with curiosity. What new plans does the universe have for me? What new person is meant to enter my life now? The flow of life is a river filled with opportunity. I allow that river to gift me with riches, to wash away my regrets, my doubts, my despair. In every loss, I see the beginning of a new unfolding. As I accept my loss, I ready myself for the hidden gift which it contains. Rather than close my heart defensively, I open my heart as a wide gate for the blessings of the world to enter.

When you really listen to yourself, you can heal yourself.

CEANNE DEROHAN

∾

THE LAMP OF INNER WISDOM
LIGHTS MY PATH

I recognize that I have a gift for insight. I salute myself for being willing to listen to my inner wisdom. I honor myself for my willingness to hold true to what I perceive even when my perceptions are not shared by those around me. In this way, I value and support my own individuality. I recognize that my perceptions are unique and trustworthy. I count my insight as a powerful blessing in my life and in the lives of those with whom I am intimate. I am tender toward myself regarding the vulnerability which my insights may engender as I willingly let go of denial and rigid and doctrinaire thinking, which is a barrier to my perceiving the truth. I bless the ever-expanding light I have to see by.

Patience is the companion of wisdom.

S T .   A U G U S T I N E

MY LIFE UNFOLDS
IN SPIRIT'S TIME

I bless Spirit's timing in my life. I surrender my sense of drama and urgency. I recognize that the slower seasons of life are necessary to find my showier and more rapid periods of expansion. I surrender my need for life to be filled with large and dramatic moments. I accept small gains, small victories. Turning away from the idea that there is some "quick fix" which will make me feel heroic and invulnerable, I accept the fact that I am a worker among workers, a friend among friends. In choosing not to force the pace of my life, I embrace wisdom over velocity.

If you read the scriptures and the philosophies, three terms
recur constantly: humility, purity, and self-control.
They say if you have these three, then you become
worthy of attaining the Truth.

SWAMI CHIDVILASANANDA

WISDOM GIVES PATIENCE TO MY SOUL

My soul is a patient traveler. I am grateful for my patient soul. Despite the temptation to think and act rashly, I root myself in the goodness of Spirit and act with temperance and wisdom. I treat myself with gentle compassion when I find myself anxious or panicky due to imagined difficulties. At all times, in all places, I remind myself that Spirit is the source of my security and that when I rest in Spirit I rest in loving companionship. In times of loneliness, when I feel misunderstood and abandoned, I allow myself to feel the presence of Spirit, guiding and supporting me, holding me safe and secure despite my fears and misgivings. I bless the path I travel with spiritual safety.

We must stop planning, plotting, and scheming and let
Infinite Intelligence solve the problem in Its own way.
God-power is subtle, silent, and irresistible. It levels
mountains and fills in valleys and knows no defeat!
Our part is to prepare for our blessings and
follow our intuitive leads.

We now give Infinite Intelligence
right-of-way.

FLORENCE SCOVEL SHINN

THE UNIVERSE IS MY
PROTECTIVE PARENT

I am a cherished child of Spirit. I am worthy to receive my blessings. I am deserving of all the benefits and blessings which enter my life. I am good and good things come to me—good people, good events, good opportunities, good lessons, good in many and multiple forms. As I accept my good, it multiplies. As I bless my good, it becomes mine in a harmonious and natural way. I enlarge my life and my life enlarges me. I expand gracefully and gently to encompass an ever more abundant life. I bless the circle of sacred safety within which I grow.

I acknowledge and declare that the Creator of all things
is now manifesting as perfection and harmony
in all my experiences.

ERNEST HOLMES

DIVINE TIMING
GUIDES MY LIFE

Divine timing guides my life. All events are unfolding for my highest good. As I seek divine will in every circumstance, I find peace, serenity, and right action. These are my blessings. I am able to enter into inner security even in the midst of outer turbulence. Reminding myself that there is an underlying flow of good in all events, I accept timing which at first may frustrate or confuse me. Knowing that I am grounded in spiritual reality, I am able to face life's circumstances with the wisdom of the long view. In every situation, the hand of grace is active for my good.

Your desire is your prayer. Picture the fulfillment of your
desire now and feel its reality and you will experience
the joy of the answered prayer.

DR. JOSEPH MURPHY

☙

I SOFTEN MY HEART TO LOVE'S TOUCH

I accept the gift of my vulnerability. I am willing to be vulnerable to love. I am willing to reveal myself in all of my human beauty and frailty. I am willing to be as I am, both perfect and a work in progress. I am willing to be unfinished, unpolished, in a state of change. I am willing to accept myself as I am and I am willing to allow others to see me as I am. I am willing to be unveiled and undefended. I am willing to be seen and understood. I am willing to view myself and others with compassion. I am willing to view myself and others nonjudgmentally. I am willing to be the human being, complete in myself without the need for accomplishment to justify my worth. Blessing myself just as I am, I lovingly open to all I can be.

Every soul is a melody which needs renewing.

STÉPHANE MALLARMÉ

MY HEARING BRINGS ME NEWS

I bless my capacity to hear the world around me. My physical sense of sound connects me to my world. The rippling sound of water, the hushed whisper of the wind, the sigh of my lover's breath, the sweet sound of a Sunday choir—all these and more are gifts to me. I focus on the sounds my hearing brings to me. I learn discernment and compassion from the tones I encounter and respond to. My hearing is acute and accurate. I am able to respond with delicacy to the subtle undercurrents revealed to me through sound.

Eating is not merely a material pleasure. Eating gives a
spectacular joy to life and contributes immensely
to goodwill and happy companionship.

ELSA SCHIAPARELLI

I SAVOR MY SENSE OF TASTE

I bless the physical gift of taste which enlivens my world. The tart taste of raspberries, the gentle taste of milk, the subtlety of spices, the crisp pungence of an apple—all flavors come to me as gifts which I enjoy. My sense of taste brings me pleasure, comfort, and connection.

I take time to savor what I eat, to appreciate the distinct flavors and exquisite shadings which food brings to my mouth. I bless my appetite and I enjoy its satisfaction. The taste of the food I eat fills me with gratitude. My life is delicious and I savor it.

Every flower is a soul blossoming in nature.

GÉRARD DE NERVAL

MY SENSE OF SMELL DEEPENS MY WORLD

The scent of newly mown grass, the smell of freshly baked bread, the aroma of pine boughs, the heady perfume of lilies—my world is filled with scents which bring me joy and comfort. The odor of freshly waxed wood, the scent of a baby's skin, the pungent smell of onions, the heady smell of autumn leaves—each of these scents brings to me a specific pleasure, a message of my benign connection to the world. I bless, too, the sense of safety conveyed to me by smell—the acrid scent of something burning, the odor of stale food that I should not eat. My sense of smell blesses me with good sense as well as with good scents.

In times of disquiet, I turn to scent to comfort me. I light a scented candle, burn a fragrant incense, mist myself with a perfume or drop of aromatic oil. My sense of smell connects me to a sense of well-being. I use it consciously and well.

I lovingly create
perfect health for myself.
My dis-ease is a valuable teacher.

LOUISE L. HAY

MY HEALTH IS A MIRROR
TO BRING ME CLARITY

In times of disease, I slow down, center myself, and focus on the blessing hidden within the circumstance. What am I meant to attend to? What grief have I ignored? What stress have I turned aside or buried? What blessing can be found by slowing down, by turning within? Disease begins as dis-ease. What can I do to ease my spirit? What blessing can I choose to encounter? A falling leaf, a spring flower, the soft drifting of a winter snow? Beautiful music, the smell of soup, the taste of a good piece of bread—all these speak to my heart, which has ears to hear them. The cleansing rain falls within as well as without. I open the ears and eyes of my heart to the abundant blessings of my natural world. I take my ease.

In a dark time, the eye begins to see.

MY PLANS AND AGENDAS ARE EXPANDED AND CORRECTED BY THE UNIVERSE

My life is blessed by grace—which acts with its own timing. In times of frustration, in times of fear, as loss and difficulty surround me, I release my plans and outcomes to the larger plans and outcomes unfolding for my benefit. Letting go of my insistence on immediate gratification, I relax into the better working-out of details and dimensions hidden from my view. Affirming that all works for the good of all if I open to the grace of co-operation, I open my heart to God's timing, God's wisdom, God's working-out of gentle benefits for all.

Listening is a form of accepting.

STELLA TERRILL MANN

⚬

I AM TEACHABLE AND HOLD A BEGINNER'S HEART

I am willing to be guided and corrected. This attitude is a great blessing. I am willing to have my thinking, my attitudes, and my actions shaped by a wisdom higher than my own. Surrendering my impatience, my doubt, and my despair, I ask, in faith, for guidance to come to me. I resolve to be of good heart and to place my life in the care of higher forces which hold toward me a benevolent and protective view. I bless the humility which opens my heart to receiving help, care, and spiritual protection.

Finally I looked within my own heart and there
I found Him——He was nowhere else.

RUMI

⬧

MY HEART LISTENS TO
THE VOICE WITHIN

My heart is fulfilled. Its yearnings are prayers preparing to be answered. The good I am seeking seeks me as well. The love I wish for is mine as I love in return. It is the nature of Spirit to give. It is my nature to receive. As I go to Spirit to fulfill my desires, I recognize that Spirit is also the source of those desires. I am a creative being. The creator within me yearns for what it wants to create. As I open myself to the divine creative energy which flows through me, I am both the prayer and its answer.

> *It is man's foremost duty to awaken the understanding of the inner Self and to know his own real inner greatness. Once he knows his true worth, he can know the worth of others. Therefore, meditate on your Self, honor and worship your own Self, kneel to your own Self, and see the Lord who is hidden in your own heart.*

SWAMI MUKTANANDA

I AM BY NATURE LOVABLE AND LOVED

I count myself as lovable. I do not need to control myself, patrol myself, or improve myself to be loved. Those who love me find me in their hearts. My lovability is not an issue. I accept the love that is offered to me and I rejoice in its appearance. I allow others to love as they are able in ways that may startle and delight me. I release my pictures of love and accept the variability of love. I allow the love in my life to be subtle, rigorous, many-colored, and multifaceted. I do not pursue love. I love by opening to love.

Committing your ways unto the Lord seems very difficult to
most people. It means, of course, to follow intuition,
for intuition is the magic path, the beeline to your
demonstration. Intuition is a Spiritual faculty above the intellect.
It is the "still small voice" commonly called a hunch,
which says, "this is the way, walk ye in it."

FLORENCE SCOVEL SHINN

I ENJOY MY OWN COMPANIONSHIP

y solitude brings me the blessing of intimacy with myself. When I am alone, I explore my own companionship, learn my own thoughts, feelings, needs, and desires. Underneath my feelings of loneliness, I sense a deeper truth: that I am companioned by the universe, that periods of solitude are periods of learning as I cock my ear and heart for guidance from higher realms. I am constantly tutored, constantly spoken to, and guided by higher forces which are universal in nature and personal in expression. Though the universe is large, I am not so small that my presence isn't noted and counted. I contain the universe within me just as the universe contains me. When I appeal to higher forces, I am appealing to the best within myself. "Lo, I contain multitudes," the poet Walt Whitman remarked. In my times of solitude, I find joy in the multitudes I contain. I bless my own nature for its riches and diversity. I am my friend.

See the world as your self.
Have faith in the way things are.
Love the world as your self;
then you can care for all things.

TAO-TE CHING

MY HEART IS CHERISHED
AND SECURE

Today I cherish the security of a love returned. I have in my life those whose friendship and devotion are assured. I reach to them and they reach to me in return. We have each other's best interests at heart. We share each other's dreams and visions of a meaningful life. I am willing to commit myself to deep and loving friendships. I am willing to take into my heart the dreams and aspirations of those I love. I am willing to support them in their dreams' unfolding. I am willing to cheer, to console, to counsel, and not compete. Taking as my guidance the rule that everyone's good prospers everyone, I am able to be a generous friend, open to the happiness and fulfillment of my friends' dreams and wishes. I am secure in the fact that as one of us moves forward we all move forward. I am able to extend myself in faith knowing I am equally and fully supported in return. As I put positive energy into the universe, the universe returns to my energy in kind.

If we face our unpleasant feelings with care, affection, and nonviolence, we can transform them into the kind of energy that is healthy and has the capacity to nourish us.

THICH NHAT HANH

I PRACTICE OPTIMISM AS A CONSCIOUS CHOICE

In times of loss and difficulty, I choose to consciously deepen my strength through actively seeking the blessing hidden in my adversity. I do not deny my painful feelings or run from them but I do choose to move through them, seeking the opportunity for insight that lies for me on the other side. I do not suffer for the sake of suffering or mistake pain as the only soil for my spiritual growth. Instead, I remind myself that suffering and pain are temporary while my spiritual comfort is eternal. Knowing this, I open my heart to the timeless comforts which Spirit provides. I take comfort in the moistening rain, in the scent of flowers, in the tall oak offering me its shade. Even when deeply troubled, I seek to find Spirit in the midst of my suffering. I soften my heart to the gentle touch of comfort. I allow Spirit to touch my grief.

We are nature.

We are nature seeing nature.

The red-winged blackbird flies in us.

SUSAN GRIFFIN

☙

I LEARN FROM THE EARTH
AND ACCEPT ITS WISDOM

The natural world is my mentor and wise companion. I bless the natural world and I allow the natural world to guide me. I allow the rain to teach me its lessons of freshness and renewal. I allow my spirit to be washed clean of any lingering doubts, angers, and anxieties. Washed by the love of Spirit, I am eager and open to undertake new growth. Quenched by divine love, I blossom ever more freely and more fully. Like the rain, I allow myself seasons. I accept loss. I accept change. I expect growth. Like the rain, I am a passing blessing on this earth. I ask that I, too, be a refreshing gift for those who encounter me, that I bless them with tenderness and leave them more refreshed.

INDEX

ABOUT THE AUTHOR

Julia Cameron is the author of fifteen books, fiction and nonfiction, and many plays and movies. She happily lives in the high desert of New Mexico where she busies herself with musicals, movies, poetry, horses, and dogs. She has taught extensively for two decades in venues ranging from London to Los Angeles, from Esalen to *The New York Times.* Her work on creativity features the best selling books *The Artist's Way, The Vein of Gold, The Right to Write,* and *God Is No Laughing Matter.*